D1446720

the sprout book

the sprout book

A CELEBRATION OF THE HUMBLE BRUSSELS SPROUT

TESS READ

Michael O'Mara Books Limited

First published in 2008 by
Michael O'Mara Books Limited
9 Lion Yard
Tremadoc Road
London SW4 7NQ

A CIP catalogue record for this book is available from the British Library.

Papers used by Michael O'Mara Books Limited are natural, recyclable products made from wood grown in sustainable forests. The manufacturing processes conform to the environmental regulations of the country of origin.

ISBN: 978-1-84317-290-1

1 3 5 7 9 10 8 6 4 2

Designed and typeset by Angie Allison

Printed and bound in Italy by L.E.G.O.

www.mombooks.com

contents

• •

dedication

To my mother, without whom this book wouldn't have been possible, and my daughter, who promises to try a Brussels sprout. One day.

introduction

. . . .

Eddie Hitler:	Not sprouts! I hate sprouts!
Richie Richard:	Oh, will you stop whinging, Eddie! *Nobody* likes sprouts.
Eddie:	Then why are we having them, then?
Richie (*screamed*):	BECAUSE IT'S CHRISTMAS!

From the episode 'Holy' in the sitcom *Bottom*, written by Rik Mayall and Adrian Edmondson

Brussels sprouts – what more do you need to say to sum up an English Christmas?

Just these two simple words and you have it all: a cold, clear winter's day, a wrapping-paper tsunami covering the carpet, Mum cooking in the kitchen, Dad drinking his way through his many presents of booze, elderly relatives trying to get a look-in (on the booze), children jealously guarding their brand-new bits of crap plastic whilst actually mindlessly watching the television, and everyone knows it's turkey, potatoes and sprouts for lunch. What could possibly be more English?

Well, the wine is made in New Zealand, the beer on the Continent, the toys in China and, of course, Brussels sprouts originally come from Brussels, in Belgium.

But, like Belgium's other much-maligned export – the Smurfs – sprouts have come to global prominence thanks to their anglicization. Sprouts are eaten all over the world because of their connection to the British Christmas.

Ironically, most British people have no idea how to cook them, so we love to whine about them; they're regularly voted Britain's most unpopular vegetable.

And not only that, but also sprouts epitomize the thing we like to whine about above all others – Christmas – so there's something about them that is utterly British. Indeed, one could argue that our upholding of the festive tradition of sprouts in the face of widespread

Q: What is the nation's favourite wine at Christmas?
A: 'Do I have to eat all my Brussels sprouts?'

11

anti-sproutism is another demonstration of that British bulldog spirit: a tenacious commitment to something against all reason. Sprouts are a perfect analogy for the whole of British culture: to learn about sprouts is to learn about ourselves.

Or something.

And in *The Sprout Book*, learn about sprouts we will.* From their distinguished history to their claims to fame, their major cultural impact to their place in chic cuisine, no leaf has been left unturned in this celebration of the humble brassica. Throughout, you'll find sprout recipes to tempt your tastebuds (honestly), as well as a host of other things to do with sprouts that you probably never thought possible.

So let's begin this voyage of discovery! Of sprouts!

A NOTE ON THE RECIPES

Some of the sprout recipes in this book can be enjoyed by people who don't like sprouts. Others, frankly, taste pretty strongly of sprouts.

For this reason, the dishes have been given a 'sproutiness rating' from 1 to 5, 5 being the sproutiest.

* chances are, by the end of the book, you'll know more about sprouts than you ever really wanted to.

so why christmas?

• •

Until we find the apostle's diary that records: 'And Jesus did say, "Thou shalt have turkey with Brussels sprouts on the side for your Christmas Day lunch and all shall be right with the world,"' we shall have to find another explanation for why Brussels sprouts became so intimately linked with Christmas.

Winter Veg

The standard theory is that sprouts are traditionally associated with Christmas because they are a hardy winter vegetable that will survive and grow through very cold weather.

An Expert Speaks

As Roger Wellberry, a major UK sprouts grower, says, 'Before freezers were invented, what other vegetable did you have for winter greens? The cauliflowers would be finished and there wasn't any broccoli in this country in those days.

'If it was a normal, cold winter, the only vegetables that would stand the cold – and that you could harvest under snow – were Brussels sprouts.'

STIR-FRIED CHRISTMAS DINNER SPROUTS WITH SOY SAUCE • *Serves 4*

This works well as an accompaniment to a traditional Christmas dinner because the crunchiness of the sprouts and the tanginess of the sauce complement the usual turkey roast.

You will need:
500 g sprouts • 2 tsp oil • Soy sauce to taste

1. Chop up the sprouts and fry them in a hot wok with a little oil for around 5 minutes.
2. Add a goodly amount of soy sauce and fry for a further minute.

STIR-FRYING SPROUTS

This recommended cooking method may sound counterintuitive, as stir-frys are usually reserved for vegetables that have at least a passing acquaintance with fare that grows in Asia – rather than the determinedly Western European sprouts.

In fact, sprouts are really delicious when stir-fried. Using this method, it's difficult to overcook them and turn them into a mushy mess.

making the most of christmas sprouts
● ●

With a reputation so intimately linked to Christmas, the potential impact of Brussels sprouts resonates far beyond the dining table.

Why not make the most of that cultural recognition? Make sprouts the key feature of your Christmas decorations with this range of fantastically original creations!

One thing's for sure: it'll set you apart from the neighbours.

The Table Centrepiece, Brussels Sprouts Style

When mentally planning the perfect Christmas, you always need to consider how your guests will perceive the art, the *enigma* that is your wintertime display.

Colours are, of course, everything. Think the green of the holly with the red of its berries. The white of snow paired with the silver of the tinsel. The intense green of Brussels sprouts with the gold of some nice new candles from Woolies.

yes – create your own table centrepiece

from sprouts and truly amaze your guests

TABLE CENTREPIECE: A HOW-TO GUIDE

Place Brussels sprouts in rows, in pyramids and/or in circles around the candles of your choice, arrange with mistletoe leaves for a seductive effect, add berries for contrast, and use your natural flare for design to maximum effect.

Sprout Candle Holders

These distinctive decorations can be placed around the home to create a softly lit environment conducive to festive fun.

CANDLE HOLDERS: A HOW-TO GUIDE

Cut the core out of one of your most choice sprouts — you know, one of those favoured ones you have given names to, like 'Sprouty' or 'Rover'. (You can wear a blindfold at this moment to lessen the pain, but it will have inevitable consequences for the end result.)

Next, mount the disembowelled sprout on to a previously prepared lake of wax with a cocktail stick sticking out of it. Mount the sprout by penetrating it with the stick (ahem).

Take a tall, thin candle and place it in the candle holder. The cocktail stick should be inserted directly into the candle, while the cored Brussels sprout gently cups it at the bottom.

Light — and enjoy the delighted gasps of your guests.

Tree Trinkets

Now we come to the Christmas tree, festooned with hanging sprouts – some painted gorgeous garish colours by the children, or indeed by you, and some as green as the day they sprouted.

To be honest, painted sprouts are better, because unless you have a silver tinsel tree – although why shouldn't you? – sprouts au naturel don't really show up against the green tree background.

For a new take on tinsel, drape Brussels Sprouts Daisy Chains (see page 101) whither you please.

> 'A lovely thing about Christmas is that it's compulsory, like a thunderstorm, and we all go through it together.'
>
> Garrison Keillor

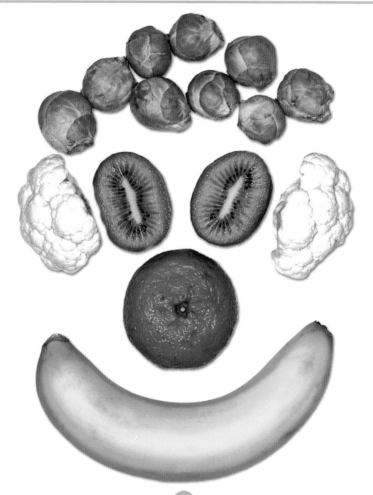

sprout party games
● ● ● ● ● ● ● ● ● ● ● ● ● ● ● ● ● ●

Perfect party games to play in
order to get rid of unwanted guests
at Christmas, or indeed any other
time of year.

Hide the Sprout

1. Hide it on day one of your
   guests arriving.
2. Tell them about it on day two.
3. If they haven't found it by day
   three, it will start smelling, giving
   them a bit of a clue.
4. Day four: if they haven't left yet,
   reveal that the sprout is hidden in their
   room, which gives them a major hint that you
   want them to leave.

The Great Chocco-Sprouto Swap

This is a truly fabulous trick to play on someone you really don't like, or indeed someone you really do like, but want to see all-but-vomit in front of their nearest and dearest.

A great trick, *if* you can hold a straight face while you do it.

BE WARNED: THIS IS DIFFICULT

You will need:

1 Brussels sprout
25 g plain chocolate
A box of ordinary chocolates

1. First, cook the sprout to within, and if possible beyond, an inch of its life. Allow it to cool.
2. Melt the chocolate – either in a glass bowl placed above a saucepan of boiling water, or in the microwave.
3. While the chocolate is at its meltiest, drop the Brussels sprout into the molten mixture and roll it around.
4. Fish it out with a spoon and leave it to set.

did you know?

Tesco's online grocery service will send you a single sprout if you ask them to.

At least, that's what they did for Howard Cooper of Stockport, who typed in '10 grams' as the quantity he wanted, rather than '100 grams'.

5. Take the box of chocolates. Insert the 'fake choc' in some prime position in the box, ensuring attention is somewhat drawn to it – if need be, by eating some of the adjacent chocolates: great art must have its foot soldiers.
6. Proffer the box of 'chocolates' to favoured, and unfavoured, guests.

in short: perform the great chocco-sprouto swap.

It may seem a lot of bother for one practical joke, but believe me, the joy of watching a highly annoying relative pause mid strident sentence to say, 'Thank you,' pick up a chocolate, resume their latest preposterous claim, only to gag suddenly and spit out slushy, mushy, green-brown Brussels sprout, preferably over an uptight ageing aunt, is genuinely worth it.

Indoor Sprouts Boules

This game is a rather fun creation, so it's best enjoyed with friends than unwanted guests.

NOTE:

Do make sure you play sprouts boules on a polished wooden floor or tiles. It's absolute crap on a carpet.

THE IDEAL VEG

Sprouts are in fact the perfect vegetable for a game of indoor boules.

They are not too big, unlike cabbages, and they are the right shape (indoor, or indeed outdoor, boules with cucumbers is a predictably unsatisfying game) because they are nearly round.

For, although tomatoes would at first glance appear to be a better boule, as they are more perfectly round and they are smooth, and thus higher speeds can be achieved than with the uneven, irregular surfaces of a Brussels sprout, it is precisely these imperfections, these uncertainties of life, that make the game the joy it is.

THE JOY OF INDOOR SPROUTS BOULES

Ah, the elation and then devastation of those moments when your Brussels sprout looks like it is on a certain path to wipe out a good friend's sprouty hopeful for the Cup, when suddenly it veers off to the left, ripped off course by an unruly outlying leaf.

The thrill of the chase, the uncertainty of the outcome, the win or lose being determined by the randomness of nature, these are the moments we live for. Such a moment is as delicious as a game of croquet on a lush green lawn on a perfect English summer's day.

CREAM-BRAISED SPROUTS

*Serves 4-6, depending on greed
and whether or not they like sprouts*

You will need:

500 g sprouts • 20 g butter • 200 ml water
300 ml single cream (full fat – reduced fat cream is
just a disaster in this recipe)

1. Prepare the sprouts by washing and removing the outer leaves.
2. Melt the butter in a large frying pan (large enough to take all the sprouts in a single layer); let it begin to 'foam' and then tip in the sprouts.

NOTE:

The purpose of Step 4 is to ensure the sprouts are cooked through. If you are really keen on crunchy sprouts, you can leave this stage out, but you'll need to braise the sprouts in the cream for longer.

3. Sauté the sprouts over a medium heat for about 5 minutes, allowing them to go through the 'bright green' stage and then get slightly browned and caramelized.
4. Add the water (it ought to come about halfway up the sprouts) and turn up the heat to maximum to bring it swiftly to the boil. Keep the sprouts bubbling away for a further 8-10 minutes, by which time most of the water will have evaporated.

5. Add the cream, reduce the heat back down to medium (the cream should be bubbling, but not briskly boiling or it will separate) and let the sprouts cook for another 15 minutes. After this time, the sprouts should be tender to the point of a sharp knife and the cream should have reduced down to a thick sauce.
6. Serve with roasted red meats.

the history of sprouts

•••

When did the earth see the first Brussels sprout? This is a matter of
fierce debate among the botanists of the world and people who care
about these sorts of things.

The Romans

The most popular theory at present has it that Brussels sprouts grew
wild in Afghanistan and Iran and the Romans brought them to Europe,
where the Belgians grew them in abundance and so they were named
after that country's capital, and the rest is history. Well, it's all history,
but you know what I mean.

Yet it's not certain that the Romans imported sprouts per se. It's the
age-old question that has troubled sprout aficionados in several fields
(see also page 82): were they truly sprouts – or merely cabbages?

Are Sprouts Really Ancient?

Were there Brussels sprouts in the ancient world or not? This is the
issue that vexes many an academic and author of small gift books on
Brussels sprouts.

Anthony Dalby's *Food in the Ancient World A-Z* says that *Brassica
Oleracea* are found in ancient nomenclature and finds references to

young cabbage sprouts. As Dalby says, 'The suggestion that it was a Brussels sprout has been scouted. Whatever it was, it was expensive.' How times change.

But prolific Roman writer Pliny described all the various varieties of cabbages he found – none of which appears to match exactly the description of Brussels sprouts.

It's a puzzler.

Simply Wizard

Some botanists are convinced that what the Romans brought over to Europe were just cabbages. They think that the Belgians achieved a 'magic mutation' to produce the wonder of sprouts, which of course makes it perfectly fair that the veggies should be named after their capital city, Brussels.

Definite Dates

The year 1587 is a special date in sprout history: it marks the first instance of a botanist recording a plant that is likely to have been a Brussels sprout. If true, this would have been the first sighting of the king of vegetables.

Thereafter, sprouts were cultivated in large volumes near Brussels. The city started growing them seriously in the seventeenth century – and then there was no stopping sprouts from achieving world domination.

sprouts around the world

At least the history of Brussels sprouts in the English-speaking world is clear.

They first appeared in English gardens and on dinner tables in the eighteenth century.

did you know?

The cookery writer Jane Grigson found the earliest English recipe for sprouts to have been written by Eliza Acton in 1845.

She suggested covering Brussels sprouts in buttery sauce and veal gravy. Mmm …

Not Born in the USA

Meanwhile, the Americans have Thomas Jefferson to thank for their sprouts – he introduced them to America by carrying them home and personally planting some in his garden in 1812.

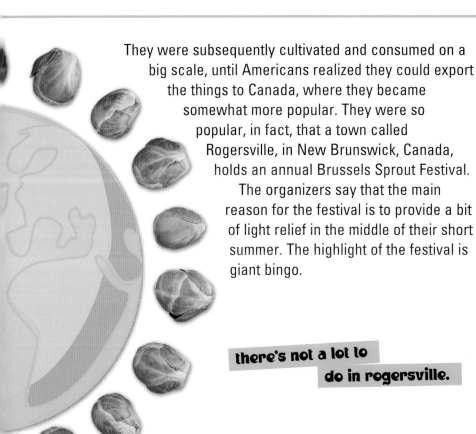

They were subsequently cultivated and consumed on a big scale, until Americans realized they could export the things to Canada, where they became somewhat more popular. They were so popular, in fact, that a town called Rogersville, in New Brunswick, Canada, holds an annual Brussels Sprout Festival. The organizers say that the main reason for the festival is to provide a bit of light relief in the middle of their short summer. The highlight of the festival is giant bingo.

there's not a lot to do in rogersville.

The Language of Sprouts

Why is it that vegetable and herb names in particular so often sound hilarious in other languages? Who among us has not laughed at finding *persil* on a French menu (parsley)? Or does not find the German word for onion, *Zwiebel*, funny?

Happily, sprouts are no exception. In French, sprouts are *chou de Bruxelles*, with *mon petit chou* being a rather unlikely term of endearment in the language. Shall I compare thee to a cabbage, indeed?

Meanwhile, Germany denies the Brussels connection altogether, by calling them merely *Rosenkohl*.

did you know?

Almost all the sprouts sold in UK shops at Christmas time are grown in the UK. The small remainder are mostly from Holland and Poland, who can probably live without them during the season of goodwill.

sprouts and belgians

• •

Bruxellians are very proud of their association with the humble sprout and are certainly convinced that one of their natives did achieve the magic mutation and that sprouts are deservedly named after their city.

Feel the Fever

The Saint-Gilles area of Brussels is where Brussels sprout fever really takes hold, where you can spot the most notable citizens by their membership of the *Confrérerie des kuulkappers* – the brotherhood of cabbage-cutters.

An Unforgettable Feast

David Rennie, the *Telegraph's* Europe correspondent, describes attending one of their annual dinners:

> For their banquet, the brotherhood dresses up in velvet robes and consumes such delights as venison with sprouts, sprouts with bacon and the *'Boulette des Kuulkappers'* (a meatball wrapped around a single sprout, like a giant savoury gobstopper).

ROASTED BUTTERNUT SQUASH AND SPROUTS • *Serves 4*

You will need:

200 g sprouts

1 butternut squash

2 cloves of garlic, chopped

400 g can of chopped tomatoes (or equivalent of fresh)

Leaves from 2 or 3 sprigs of rosemary

1. Chop the bases off the sprouts, then put the sprouts to one side.
2. Peel and then cut the butternut squash in half, removing all the seeds and gooey stuff and putting that in the bin. Chop the remaining hard flesh of the squash into small cubes and fry with the garlic in a large saucepan over a medium heat, until the squash flesh is soft (roughly 15-20 minutes).
3. Add the tin of chopped tomatoes.*
4. Toss in the sprouts. Give the mixture a good stir and then pour it straight into an oven dish.
5. Sprinkle the top with rosemary. Roast it all in the oven (preheated to 180°C) for 20-25 minutes.
6. Serve with seasonal vegetables and mashed potatoes.

* you can use fresh tomatoes instead, but if you do, you should remove the skins and as many of the seeds as possible. the amount of tomato you are left with is so pitiful as to make you think it's hardly worth it, and indeed for the sake of this recipe it almost certainly isn't.

selling the sprout

In today's media-savvy, ultra-competitive commercial markets, the humble sprout can't afford to rest on its laurels. It must be taken to the front line to pitch for its place on dinner tables across the globe, with slogans and sales targets now a real part of its daily life.

M is for Marketing

Where does the marketing budget come from for sprouts, I hear you ask? From the Brussels Sprouts Growers' Association, set up by Syngenta, which is the UK's biggest seller of Brussels sprout seeds, as well as other sprout growers. It's a dog-eat-dog world in modern greengrocery.

A Sprout Is For Life, Not Just For Christmas

Or so the advertising agency for sprouts said, who came up with that line in 2004.

(Proof once again that advertising isn't always a glamour job.)

Other sprout-tastic slogans include 'Learn to Love a Sprout' from 2006, which was judged to have reached 80 million consumers.

Taking Sprouts to the Masses

In 2004, the unforgettable TV series *Sexing Up the Sprout* was launched.

Broadcast on UKTV Food, it was fronted by 'housewives' favourite' chef James Martin, who was encouraged to produce original and innovative sprouty recipes. His most enduring were the Sprout Egg – a Scotch egg with a sprout inside – and the Sproutini.

(This last one is frankly a bit of a cheat in my opinion, as it's just a normal martini with a frozen sprout in it instead of an olive.)

Worth Their Weight in Sprouts

The advertising campaigns certainly worked their magic: sprout sales reached a peak of £48m per year.

This equates to some 35,000 tonnes of sprouts grown in the UK each year, which means that between us we eat around 4,800,000,000 individual sprouts. I think we can all agree that that's a lot of sprouts.

We All Love Sprouts ...

With figures like that, it's no surprise to discover that we are all sprout aficionados really, as (according to a survey conducted for the 'Learn to Love a Sprout' campaign) 75 per cent of Britons eat sprouts and 81 per cent of us cook with them.

... Or Do We?

Though we could put it another way: a survey that was paid for by growers of Brussels sprouts found that people like sprouts. If they had been growers of broccoli, what do you think they would have found?

Of course, this is all in a good cause, because we should eat local British produce and we should eat our greens.

All I'm saying is that if next week you read in the paper that 'Survey shows that slightly rotted horse manure is incredibly popular with 85 per cent of households,' do wonder who paid for it.

A Sprout Is For Christmas, Not For Life

Unfortunately, research reveals that the 2004 advertising slogan was bollocks.

While the Brussels Sprouts Growers' Association and their ad agency would like to pretend that sprout popularity is otherwise, the chief salad and vegetable buyer for Waitrose has his head screwed on and knows that if he filled his shop with sprouts all year round, he'd have eleven months' worth of rotting unsold sprouts on his hands.

As columnist Katherine Whitehorn observed:

'From a commercial point of view, if Christmas did not exist, it would be necessary to invent it.'

The Decline and Fall of the British Sprout

Sadly, despite the best efforts of housewives' favourite chefs and advertising agencies, the sprout in fact remains a vegetable in long-term decline.

The overall acreage under sprout cultivation in the UK has fallen from 20,000 acres in 1998 to around 15,000 acres in 2008. In the government's 'average shopping basket index', sprouts have given way to broccoli and sat navs.

Since a Sprout Egg and a Sproutini contain only one sprout per serving, it's hard to predict a massive turnaround in sprout demand.

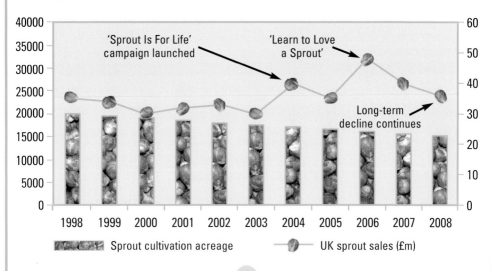

did you know?

Thomas Cook, the travel agents, became the enemies of sprout lovers everywhere in 2001 when they created an advert featuring a bowl of sprouts and the caption: 'It's time to get away.'

The idea being that if you took a Christmas mini-break, you wouldn't have to eat sprouts.

The British Sprout Growers' Association demanded an apology on behalf of sprout growers and eaters everywhere ... but didn't get one.

sprouts can save the planet

Why not take inspiration from the colour of sprouts? Go green – and revolutionize your planet-saving efforts in the home with this versatile vegetable.

Indeed, sprouts can provide not only the inspiration for your Christmas, but also the insulation of it.

ENDORSED BY EXPERTS

The UK's loft lobbying corporation has agreed – it's amazing what you can do with a few sprouts.

Sadly, they also concurred with the results of our experiments: it's all a bit of a wasted effort, as you do have to replace the entire sprout collection after a week or two when they start going soft. And mouldy.

Sprout Insulation

It is possible to derive some surprisingly good loft insulation from Brussels sprouts.

Packed together tightly and cut cleverly so as to be well tessellated, the compacted sprouts will form a strong bond insulating you from the chill winter winds and from the noise of passing revellers on the pavement below.

Burn Sprouts, Not Coal

If only the miners had thought of it. Why take canaries into lifts to dig black stuff out of the earth when you can just grow a perfectly good replacement in your garden?

Sprouts are dense, compact, and although they don't burn odourlessly, the smell isn't quite as bad as you might think.

Top tip if you do decide to burn sprouts: add some orange peel to your warming winter fire after you've lit the sprouts, so that your guests don't vomit from the stench.

(Unless you actively want to get rid of your guests, of course, in which case turn to page 23 for the perfect party games to get them running for the hills.)

did you know?

It is possible to make diesel biofuel from Brussels sprouts scrapings. But this is probably not an efficient use of anyone's time or money.

Q: What's green and goes camping?
A: A cub sprout.

45

SPROUT AND POTATO CAKES
Serves 4-6

**SPROUTINESS
RATING: 2/5**
This dish is not very
sprouty because it's
not overly evident that
what's behind the cakes'
crunch is sprouts.

You will need:
500 g potatoes
500 g sprouts
2 tsp oil
A potato ricer

1. Boil the potatoes for 15 minutes,
   then mash. Reserve.
2. Cut the bases off the sprouts. Lightly
   boil the Brussels for around
   7 minutes, until they are al dente.
3. Chop the sprouts into pieces
   and combine them with the
   mashed potatoes.
4. Make hamburger-sized
   cakes from the mixture.

5. Fry the cakes gently in a little oil. Turn them over when one side is browned.
6. Serve with seasonal vegetables such as mange tout or carrots.

you can even add a parsley sauce if you are feeling adventurous.

sprouts: the marmite effect

Sprouts divide people. They are repeatedly voted Britain's most unpopular vegetable – and yet they are adored by many. It's the Margaret Thatcher syndrome, or in taste terms: the Marmite effect.

Are You Or Have You Ever Been ... ?

However, unlike with Marmite, there is a sort of shame attached to liking sprouts – it is the modern love that dare not speak its name.

People like to say they don't like sprouts – and the more metrosexual somewhere is, the fewer people own up to eating them. Londoners, for

did you know?

There is a genetic reason why some people like sprouts and others hate them.

Sprouts contain compounds called glucosinolates, which are bitter tasting. Although these bitter compounds are broken down by cooking, they remain present. Geneticists have discovered that about 30 per cent of people have a genetic idiosyncrasy that means they can't detect this bitterness.

So, the theory goes that if you have the idiosyncrasy, you will like sprouts, and if you don't, you won't.

example, eat fewer sprouts than Devonians (70 per cent of London chomps away, compared to 85 per cent of the Southwest).

'Son, it's time we told you. There are some people in this world who don't LIKE Brussels sprouts...'

Sprouts: It's Time to Take Sides

The Brussels sprout is a subject on which everyone has an opinion. Are you for or against?

Pro-Sprout
In the green corner, the following are lining up to proclaim their love of sprouts.

Musician **Nick Cave** freely admitted to the *Telegraph* in 2007 that he is a 'fish fingers and Brussels sprouts kind of guy. I fry them all at the same time.'

Cherie Booth and **Jo Brand** have published recipes to prove their pro-sprout credentials … in top cookery tomes such as *Hello!* magazine.

Kate Winslet is such a huge sprouts fan that, when she was filming the movie *Holy Smoke* in Australia, seeing Brussels sprouts made her suddenly homesick. She just had to have them. 'I went in, I saw Brussels sprouts – they were massive – and I just really wanted them.'

Alan Davies, notorious *QI* comedian and, allegedly, tramp ear-biter is a sprouts fan: 'I love them steamed, and sometimes, post-steam, I stir-fry them with a bit of curry powder. Lush, if a bit trumpy.' Indeed.

It's sprouts all the way for Bolton Wanderers' leftfield striker **El-Hadji Diouf**. According to *The Bolton News*, he 'swears by a portion of Brussels sprouts' to keep him fit.

American actress **Mischa Barton**, meanwhile, reveals the reason she holidays in Britain: 'I love all the mashed potatoes, the mushy peas and Brussels sprouts. And oh my god, Cadbury's chocolate! It is so much better than Hershey's which we have in America.' The acting's better, too.

we love sprouts

Anti-Sprout

Nicholas Hoult of the hit drama *Skins* has told the nation that he 'won't eat Brussels sprouts, but I'm always forced to eat my greens at home'.

Jenny McAlpine, otherwise known as Fiz Brown in *Coronation Street*, eschews the glamorous Granada soap scene at Christmas and returns home to Lancashire for her dad's cooking: 'We have all the traditions that you don't really like, but that you're supposed to have at Christmas, like Brussels sprouts.'

American writer **P. J. O'Rourke** is anti-veg, not just anti-sprouts, it seems: 'A fruit is a vegetable with looks and money. Plus, if you let fruit rot it turns into wine, something Brussels sprouts never do.'

Bear Grylls. Actual adventurer. He's the man you've seen on *Man versus Wild*, extolling the virtues of termites or jumping into frozen lakes, building rafts to escape from islands, and so on. He's not a fan of camel hump.

'Camel hump was bad – they store 95 per cent of their fat in their hump. I was getting the skin off so I could use it as a blanket, and I tried some of the fat and, really, it was one of the few times I vomited on the show.'

He is also not keen on goats' testicles: 'They're the size of baseballs, but as soon as I put them in my mouth, they just melted with cold sperm. It was one of my low points.'

But, when asked his least favourite food, it is no contest: 'Brussels sprouts. Brussels sprouts are the devil.'

Does he actually prefer raw goats' testicles to Brussels sprouts? 'Definitely.'

we hate sprouts

Gardeners' Question Time Joins the Debate

This exchange was broadcast on Radio 4 on 25 November 2007.

Audience member: My wife and I are growing vegetables and our favourite vegetable is the Brussels sprout. [...]

Peter Gibbs: I've not heard that sentence very often, 'My favourite vegetable is the Brussels sprout!' Although I must admit I'm quite partial to them myself.

Note here how Peter Gibbs shows off the classic shame a sprout-lover feels. He knows that conventional wisdom has it that we all hate sprouts, but reluctantly admits he is himself partial to them.

If this book has but one message, it is:

speak out your **love** of sprouts!

be not ashamed!

hide not your love for this

greenest of green little

vegetabley ball of

goodness!

the art of cooking sprouts

....

'Right now look, there's only five hours until lunch,
I've got to get my sprouts on. Don't want them all crunchy.'

Richard Richard in *Bottom*, written by Rik Mayall and Adrian
Edmondson

....

There are many and fierce debates about how to cook Brussels sprouts,
and specifically about how to make them taste nice. There is a theory
advanced that the reason so many people, and all children the world
over, dislike sprouts is because they have never had them cooked
properly.

Conventional Cooking

After all, the historical way of preparing sprouts was to cook them for so
long that the resulting mess hovered in agonizing indecision between
slime and mush. The Christmas turkey was cooked overnight for about
nine hours – and so the sprouts were too.

And the error wasn't only made at Christmas. Every Sunday, people
would overcook their brassicas as per this 'Traditional Northern Sprouts'
recipe.

TRADITIONAL NORTHERN SPROUTS
Serves 6-8, plus one disgusting uncle

You will need:
1 kg sprouts • 3 litres water

1. Prepare the sprouts by washing and removing the loose outer leaves.
2. Cut a cross into the base of each sprout so that the flavour can leach out more easily, and so that the boiling water can get right into the heart of each sprout.
3. Bring the water to a boil in the largest iron saucepan in the house.
4. Tip the sprouts into the boiling water and go to church. After the sprouts have been boiling for three hours, check them.

THE TASTE TEST

For really traditional sprouts, the rule of thumb has always been that if you can count them, they're not done.

For a more modern dish of sprouts, reflecting the progress in English cooking over the last twenty years, you can leave them with a little more texture — it should be possible to cut them with a wooden spoon.

5. Strain the sprouts, reserving as much of the cooking water as possible to be drunk at a later date by your most revolting uncle (who will correctly note that all the goodness from the sprouts has gone into the water, although may not quite understand that it has then been destroyed by three hours' boiling).

6. Serve with a delicious roast and unaccountably perfect Yorkshire pudding. Do not leave the table until you have finished your sprouts.

'Brussels sprouts turned Grandma's dinners into something spooky and surreal. My grandfather grew everything to a huge size, and with the Brussels sprouts he insisted ... that when he went out to the pub in the morning at 10.30 a.m. they were put on to boil, and they were still boiling when he came back at 3.30 p.m. When they hit the plate, they resembled something like a slime mould.'

Chris Beardshaw, *Gardeners' Question Time*, Radio 4

the truth about sprouts

Amidst all these nasty memories lying like sprout leaves about the compact heart of the sprouts themselves, is the core, the kernel of truth about sprouts: if you haven't eaten them since childhood, chances are you have never eaten them cooked properly. So, all we are saying is …

Sprout Salvation

give sprouts a chance.

This book offers the controversial opinion that if you cook sprouts well, they don't produce that horrible sulphurous smell remembered from every childhood, and they are not flabby and vile.

Instead, they can have a lovely, nutty, meaty taste and a satisfying bite to them – like good, fresh, just-cooked-right broccoli.

did you know?

An annual Brussels Sprouts Festival is held each October. The first was hosted by Chipping Campden and sponsored by Syngenta, the UK's biggest seller of Brussels sprout seeds.

Sprouts' Secret Weapon

In Worcestershire, not too far from the sprouty stamping grounds of Chipping Campden, there is a restaurant that goes under the name of the Fusion Brasserie. Its chef patron is Italian-born Felice Tocchini. Felice is a true sprout believer.

He has developed a series of recipes that put sprouts in never-before-seen places, with truly remarkable results.

Creating a Craze for Sprouts

For instance, so successful has his 'Sprouty Cake' been with his restaurant customers, he's now looking at scaling out the product to other suppliers. A local bakery has already expressed interest and the cake was showcased at the Good Food Show in 2004.

His Sprout Ice Cream and Sprout Soufflé, meanwhile, are receiving rave reviews from his regulars, while kids go crazy for his Sprouty Muffins and Sprouty Fairy Cakes.

Felice says, 'These cakes are sweet and 95 per cent of children won't know they're eating vegetables.' Ay, that's the way to do it – truth be damned.

DIY Sprout Dishes

Felice is dead keen on spreading love for sprouts and you'll find his recipes dotted throughout.

try them, they're good. honestly.

FELICE TOCCHINI'S
SPROUTY CAKE • *Makes 1 cake*

You will need:
For the cake:
125 g carrots • 125 g sprouts • 40 g walnuts • 2 eggs
125 g sugar • 100 ml vegetable oil • 125 g self-raising flour
1/2 tsp cinnamon • 1/2 tsp fresh ginger, grated
1/2 tsp vanilla essence • 30 g raisins • 25 g dried coconut

For the frosting (optional):
25 g natural yoghurt • 150 g icing sugar

1. Line a 2-lb baking tin with greaseproof paper. Preheat the oven to 180°C.
2. Grate the carrots, and chop the sprouts and walnuts. Reserve.
3. Beat the eggs, sugar and oil together for a couple of minutes, then add the flour, cinnamon, ginger and vanilla essence. Carry on mixing for another minute.
4. Fold in the carrots, sprouts, walnuts, raisins and dried coconut.
5. Pour the cake mix into the prepared tin and cook in the oven for 50 minutes to an hour, until you can insert a toothpick in the middle and it comes out dry.

6. Once cooled, the cake can either be served just as it is, or you can enrich it by decorating with a natural yoghurt frosting. Combine the yoghurt and icing sugar and mix well for at least 6 or 7 minutes with a wooden spoon, then spread the frosting on top of the sponge.

sprouts are the new black

And so, discreetly but deftly, sprouts have shimmied their way into twenty-first-century haute cuisine.

Shane Osborn, head chef at London's Michelin-starred Pied à Terre restaurant – and thus an actual foodie hero whose word on sprouts should be trusted – is one of the modern wave of chef sprout enthusiasts.

From Bad Beginnings ...

As usual, Shane's introduction to sprouts was as a kid.

'My mum used to steam them – that is the worst way of cooking them – they would go all grey and there would be this stench through the house when I came home from school, which was not at all appealing.

'So the battle with sprouts is to get over that barrier of people's dreadful childhood memories of them; it sticks in their minds like tapioca pudding.'

... To A Flavorsome Finish

Since becoming a chef, Shane has discovered different ways of treating sprouts and is now a convert.

'Sprouts can be a really lovely vegetable, if they are cooked right. We've been using them for about four or five years; in the restaurant we sauté them with smoked bacon, partridge and pheasant.

'We've had a lot of feedback from people saying they have never seen them cooked that way before, but they're lovely. People are reluctant to try them, but when they do, they love them.'

SHANE OSBORN'S SPROUT GAZPACHO

One recipe Shane has to avoid a recreation of those childhood memories is this.

1. Shave the Brussels sprouts very finely on a mandolin.*
2. Boil them for a few minutes, then add to a velouté base.*
3. Purée the combination very quickly and chill to keep the greenness and freshness.

* technical note: a 'mandolin' is a kind of slicing machine and a 'velouté base' is a veal stock thickened with flour.

shane, as we have mentioned, is a world-class michelin-starred chef and tends to use terms like this on the assumption that everyone else will know what he means.

cross the bottom?

To cross or not to cross? Gordon Ramsay says it makes them fall apart, while Nigella Lawson says she can't help herself, she has to cross sprouts.

A Michelin-Starred Chef Speaks

Shane Osborn says, 'A lot of people make the mistake of putting a cross in the bottom. This doesn't work – it helps the cooking a bit, but sprouts are so compact that a simple cross can't cook the middle of the sprout without making the outer leaves mushy and horrible.'

This message doesn't seem to have got through to us: according to a recent survey, over two thirds of people questioned said that they put a cross in the bottom of sprouts before cooking them.

Rebels Without a Cross

Intriguingly, the further north you live, the less likely you are to cross your sprouts: only 53 per cent of Scots cross their sprouts, while 70 per cent of those in London and the Southeast do.

Let's Examine the Evidence

What this survey didn't point out – presumably because it was a piece
of sprouty analysis too far – is that the further north you live,
the less likely you are to cross your sprouts and the more likely you
are to eat, and therefore presumably like, them. A connection?

the sprout colour chart

Bright leafy green – the colour of sprouts that have been very briefly steamed, or sautéed in butter for a short while. Delicious, although perhaps a bit too crunchy for some people.

Slightly duller green – the colour of raw sprouts. It takes a genuine culinary hard nut to eat raw sprouts, although they can be nice shredded into a salad.

Gentle pistachio – the colour of braised or lightly steamed sprouty perfection.

 Sulphurous greeny-yellow – these sprouts are overcooked. Potentially still edible if they have been cooked slowly with bacon and chestnuts, but well on the way to sogginess.

 Dull khaki – horrible. The cut-with-a-spoon sprouts of childhood, known and hated the world over.

 Black – burnt sprouts.

FELICE TOCCHINI'S SPROUT CANAPÉS • *Serves 6*

You will need:

400 g large sprouts, trimmed
100 g chestnuts, cooked and peeled
2 tbsp sour cream
40 g mature cheddar, grated
Salt and pepper
Red and yellow pepper, sliced thinly, for decoration

1. Cook the sprouts in boiling salted water for 2 minutes. Then remove from the hot water and dip into cold water.
2. Scoop out the centre of each sprout.
3. Crush the chestnuts and combine with the sour cream and cheddar. Season to taste.
4. Fill the centre of the sprouts with the mixture, and then decorate with some of the peppers.

the nutritious sprout

Sprouts are good for you. There's no two ways about it.

Unless, that is, you have thyroid problems, in which case the compounds in them (and other vegetables like broccoli), called glucosinolates, are (mildly) toxic to you.

These very same compounds are the ones that potentially stave off cancer in healthy people (see page 88). So sprouts really are the ultimate kill or cure.

The Hard Facts and Figures

If they don't kill you, they're good for you. But just how good?

A single serving of Brussels sprouts, typically containing about four sprouts, will have you consuming:

vitamin	% of recommended daily amount
Vitamin A	8 per cent
Vitamin C	120 per cent
Vitamin K	243 per cent

So, you will have overdosed on vitamin K to the tune of 143 per cent – but apparently this is OK.

Thy Cup Overflow'th

Some (for 'some', read 'mothers') believe that four sprouts is insufficient really to be considered 'a serving', and instead insist that you need to go for a full cup, which research has shown is more like five or six Brussels sprouts.

With a full cup of sprouts, you also get a whopping 4 grams of fibre, an astonishing 3.98 grams of protein (good for all those vegans out there) and other goodies such as iron, potassium and calcium.

the sprout diet

●●●●●●●●●●●●●●●●●●●●●●●●●●●●●●●●●●●

While it's true that sprouts are full of healthy goodness, this doesn't mean that you should subsist wholly on them. But that didn't stop a certain someone from trying …

Geraint Benney

Welshman Geraint Benney is a striking individual. He's a bald Elvis impersonator, who styles his act 'Elvis Preseli' (say it in a real 'Welsh Valleys' voice and you have the joke). He's stood in a bona fide political election as a Plaid Cymru candidate. He's also an actor with several roles under his belt.

But the reason Geraint has a unique place in *The Sprout Book* is because of his most notorious claim to fame: he is the creator of the Sprout Diet.

The Diet Plan

The Sprout Diet does what it says on the tin. You eat just sprouts: for breakfast, lunch and dinner. Solely sprouts.

The sprout-induced lunacy sees followers carrying around raw sprouts in their pockets to consume as snacks between meals. Geraint even drank 'sprouts water' – the water drained off from boiling sprouts – as 'cocktails'.

He Practised What He Preached

Mr Benney is no experience-shy evangelist. He has actually tried his culinary creation.

And the results? Well, the Sprout Diet did make him lose weight; he lost a stone and a half in two months. But I suspect that it may have made him lose a few friends too – as there have to be some pretty serious consequences for your digestion from eating Brussels sprouts 24/7.

did you know?

Geraint used to style himself 'Sproutman' and appeared on Channel 4's *The Big Breakfast* to promote his sprouty way of life.

SUPER-EASY ROASTED SPROUTS WITH BACON AND CHESTNUTS
Serves 4

These are best served with seasonal vegetables
and rice, potatoes or another carbohydrate.

You will need:
500 g sprouts • 6 rashers of streaky bacon
100 g sweet chestnuts • Pinch of nutmeg

1. Preheat the oven to 160°C. Chop up the sprouts and bacon into small
   pieces. Put them and the chestnuts into an oven dish and sprinkle
   with nutmeg.
2. Roast in the oven for 20-25 minutes, until lightly browned.

This recipe can be summarized thus:
1. Put everything in dish.
2. Cook in oven.
3. Er …
4. That's it.

changing sprouts

• •

Why spend money on expensive home makeovers when you can just use Brussels sprouts?

Sprouts can provide a beautiful backdrop not only for the Christmas season, but the whole year round. This could be the original home décor solution you've been searching for.

Sprout Stencils

Take the simple shape of a Brussels sprout and create a stencil from its ever-lovely form.

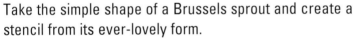

Then, using alternate pale green and a more vibrant, expressive – dare one say it, sprouty – kind of green, paint your stencils on the walls of your kitchen, your front door, even your bedroom …

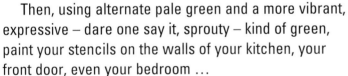

Curtain Poles and Curtain Finials

Why are fancy curtain poles and their ending cousins, finials, so expensive? It's approaching something of a crime in our modern society that you can't buy a decent multi-layered distressed cream-and-gold wooden curtain pole with gold-painted artichoke finials on each end for less than 40 quid. It's an outrage.

But, happily, one that sprouts can cure. Here's how.

A HOW-TO GUIDE

1. Take a particularly long, and hopefully relatively straight, sprout stalk. There's your curtain pole. Now paint it cream, then wait a couple of days. Then paint it gold. Wait again.

2. Now take a butter knife (not your literal butter knife, obviously. This is just a builder's turn of phrase, as I have learned through experience) and scrape — not too fiercely, not too gently — along the stalk.

78

Repeat ad nauseam. Either the stalk will be distressed by the end of the experience, or you will be.

3. For the finials, take a simple wooden doorknob, and a choice sprout. Go to your nearest art shop and buy a small crafting wood knife, then sculpt the piece of wood into the precise shape and image of the sprout.

beautiful! i'm sure you will agree.

If, however, it isn't, you might consider that 40 quid isn't so much an outrage as well worth the cash.

Brussels Sprouts Doorstops

It is possible to join some Brussels sprouts together with superglue (or honey, for a more natural alternative that doesn't really work), moulding them into a solid shape suitable to be used as a doorstop.

For the finishing touch, lacquer your Brussels sprout mountain with clear varnish – Dulux Diamond may be the best product for this purpose.

However, the sprouts will still go rotten on the inside, so it's not really worth the effort for the few weeks it will last before the maggots start appearing. Unless you're thinking of it as a Christmas present for someone you don't like (see Christmas Presents for People You Don't Like, page 102).

The Ultimate Room Centrepiece:
The Brussels Sprout Chandelier

Who needs crystal when you have sprouts?

Take your regular chandelier, and supplant some of those annoying shiny crystally things hanging down with God's own sprouts. Green and matt as nature intended. Ay truly: ding dong merrily on high.

As always, remember to take them down after a few days before the mould appears.

sprouts in art

The first recorded Brussels sprout in art hangs resplendent in the National Gallery of Scotland in a painting currently titled *The Cromartie Fool*. The portrait was painted by Richard Waitt in 1731.

The Name Game

The wonderfully evocative title is a relatively recent one for the painting. When it first arrived at the National Gallery of Scotland, it was rather more prosaically called *Gardener Holding a Cabbage with a Candle*, which not only leaves out the fool aspect, but crucially denies the Brussels sprout element.

Cabbage or Sprout?

Professor Dixon, of the University of Strathclyde's Department of Bioscience and Biotechnology, believes that the Cromartie fool's plant may well be not a cabbage, as it had been entitled, but an early type of Brussels sprout.

His evidence for this is that the artist has depicted both leaf scars (where buds/sprouts have been removed) and also secondary growth coming from auxiliary buds.

And Not Only That ...

Moreover, and a point that was of considerable interest to Professor Dixon, as indeed it would be to anyone with even a passing interest in plant diseases in art, he believes that the root system seems to show swellings indicative of infection by clubroot.

If, as we hardly dare to hope, this is so, it would be the first time clubroot was depicted in art.

Subsequent Depictions

Later examples – I am sure I need not remind the reader – have been seen in some of the globe's most famous paintings, such as *Déjeuner sur l'Herbe avec un Depiction de Clubroot Aussi* and *The Boyhood of Raleigh with Clubroot in Background*, and *Mona Lisa with a Clubfoot*.

The last may not be strictly accurate, in either respect.

A Fool's Ritual

Meanwhile, the really intriguing bit is why the Cromartie fool was holding up a long Brussels sprout stalk in the first place: it was because it was used as a 'kail-runt' torch, which was a key element in the rituals that went on around Halloween in those days.

Slightly less exciting than they sound, 'kail-runt' torches were early attempts at lighting vegetables at Halloween. History will record that turnips were more successful than sprouts, and pumpkins more successful than turnips.

FELICE TOCCHINI'S TWICE-BAKED SPROUT SOUFFLÉ

Makes 7 ramekin-sized baby soufflés

You will need:

200 ml milk • 25 g butter
1/4 small onion, finely chopped
1/2 small clove of garlic, finely chopped • 375 g sprouts, finely sliced
40 g plain flour • 2 eggs (separated, whites stiffly beaten)
165 g cheddar cheese, grated • 1/2 tsp nutmeg
Salt and pepper, pinch of each • 25 ml whipping cream

1. Grease and flour seven ramekin dishes, then tap the ramekins upside down to remove any excess flour. Preheat the oven to 180°C.
2. Put the milk on to boil. At the same time, in a separate pan, melt the butter over a low heat.
3. Add the onion and garlic to the butter and cook gently until golden.
4. Throw in the sprouts and carry on cooking on a low heat for 5 minutes.
5. Add the flour and mix well, then cook gently for 2 more minutes, mixing constantly.
6. Remove from the heat and stir in the boiling milk to form a thick béchamel; cook for a few more minutes.

7. Remove from the heat again and add the egg yolks, 125 grams of the cheese, the nutmeg and some seasoning. Mix well.
8. Carefully fold in the egg whites, then pour the mixture into the prepared ramekins.
9. Cook in a bain-marie (an ovenproof dish filled with water, which should come about halfway up the ramekins) in the oven for 20–25 minutes, or until risen and golden.
10. Remove from the oven. Let the soufflés cool down enough for you to handle, before removing each soufflé from its ramekin. You might need to run a knife around the edge to facilitate the soufflé coming out.
11. Place the upturned soufflés in an ovenproof dish. Pour a little cream over each one and scatter the remaining cheddar on top. Put the dish back in the oven for a few more minutes to gratinate, before serving.

WARNING:
SOUFFLÉS ARE DIFFICULT,
EVEN SPROUTY ONES.

sprouts: a health q & a

It seems that people have been making dubious and exaggerated health claims about sprouts for as long as there have been sprouts.

But let's get real here. Most people who regularly eat sprouts (i.e. not just at Christmas) have a pretty healthy lifestyle overall. How many people do you know who smoke twenty a day, drink eight pints at a session, gorge themselves on burgers and chips, but who also put away a man-sized serving of sprouts a couple of times a week? Not many.

Eating a lot of green vegetables is good for you. Sprouts are a green vegetable. So, we could leave it at that – but while we're on the subject, let's take a moment to find out some more facts.

Do sprouts make your hair curly?

No. After hours of diligent research, nobody in the agricultural, medical, gastronomical or hairdressing professions has the slightest idea how this obvious old wives' tale ever got off the ground.

Can sprouts cure cancer?

Yes, probably a bit, but it would be unwise to rely on them as your only therapy.

Surely you're having me on?

Since sprouts are green and strong-tasting – and dimly associated with childhood memories of your mum saying, 'Eat them up they're good for you' (insert accent of your choice) – it is no surprise that they are big news with alternative health enthusiasts.

The fact that sprouts make you fart (actual scientific fact, see page 127) only endears them further to the kind of person who believes that picking through your own poo is a good idea.

And so, while readers of a sceptical turn of mind might be forgiven for casting something of a baleful glance at the claim that sprouts cure cancer, which is commonly made over the Internet and in a thousand little badly-typeset pamphlets, it appears that – surprise, surprise! – this seemingly unlikely assertion does have at least a grain of truth to it.

Where's the evidence?
In a study carried out at the University of Leicester, it was found that a chemical called indome-3-carbinol had the effect of killing off cancer cells. Sprouts are the most concentrated natural source of indole-3-carbinol there is.

so, hooray for sprouts!

Well, maybe not so fast, because:
- The amount of indole-3-carbinol used was equivalent to an awful lot of sprouts, specifically a shopping trolley full of them, which I think even sprout lovers would agree is an *awful lot of sprouts*.
- The sprout extract was used alongside normal chemotherapy chemicals.
- It is not yet clear whether the performance of indole-3-carbinol in a lab will translate across to the more relevant case of sprouts in the tum.

Is that the only proof?

No, there's more. Sproutological research is a big thing in cancer studies at the moment, though we're only scratching the surface of it here. Thank goodness.

A study in the Netherlands investigated the theory that sulforaphane – one of the chemicals that makes sprouts taste sprouty – stimulates the liver to produce enzymes that are known to neutralize some of the damage caused by carcinogenic chemicals.

The Dutch team proved that this was a genuine effect by feeding five healthy* men a diet that included 10 oz of cooked sprouts every day for three weeks, and found that they had a 28 per cent decrease in measured DNA damage by the end of the study.**

Of course, there are a few caveats here too:

- Although less DNA damage ought to mean less risk of cancer, nobody's actually proved that the sprouts–cancer connection works directly.
- Ten ounces (300 grams) of sprouts every day for three weeks is a hell of a lot of sprouts.

* presumably strappingly so in a hugely tall kind of dutch way, but the researchers didn't actually reveal this.
** dna damage is a normal thing, by the way, despite the way it sounds.

Is celebrating the health benefits of sprouts a recent trend?

By no means. The ancients' respect for the medicinal properties of the cabbage family was significant – for example, they propagated the theory that people suffering from dysentery should eat boiled cabbage sautéed in olive oil. (You might think that if you had dysentery you were in a bad enough way anyhow without needing boiled cabbage to add to your woes.)

Plus there was a famous recipe for cabbages that had an 800-year vogue for its supposed ability to prevent drunkenness and cure gout.

Any other dubious health claims regarding sprouts?

Well, there is one. You can easily turn a few Brussels sprouts into a soothing ice treatment, providing comfort for sore eyes, sprains and bruises.

Tired eyes can get instant relief. Simply pop one frozen Brussels sprout into each eye socket.

(Interestingly, you can also get a similar effect from frozen pebbles. Hot pebbles are also very soothing, but getting them that way is more tricky. Do not try hot Brussels sprouts on the eyes, by the way, it's just sticky and horrid.)

BRAISED SPROUTS WITH APPLE AND BACON
Serves 4

In general, slow cooking is the death of sprouts – it breaks down the sulphur compounds that give them their flavour and leaves them mushy and disgusting.

But rules are there to be broken. As with other members of the cabbage family, long, slow cooking with bacon and apple, plus a few seasonings, can leave sprouts tender and delicious.

This dish goes particularly well with a Sunday roast.

You will need:

500 g sprouts • 100 g streaky bacon • 1 cooking apple
1 tsp brown sugar • 1 tsp juniper berries • 175 ml white wine or cider

1. Preheat the oven to 150°C.
2. Prepare the sprouts by washing them and removing loose leaves.
3. Cut the bacon into thin strips the size of matchsticks and peel, core and chop the apple.
4. Put the sprouts into a large ovenproof casserole dish with a lid. Mix in the bacon, sugar, juniper berries and chopped apple.

5. Pour the wine or cider over the concoction, put the lid on and place in the oven.
6. Cook for 30 minutes, then remove the lid and place back in the oven for a further 5 minutes, to reduce the liquid before serving.

the name's sprout, russell sprout

A council tax officer from Southampton has legally changed his name to Russell Sprout.

He had been Russell James Bridges, but was always nicknamed 'Sprout' because of his first name. When his friends dared him to change his surname to Sprout, it was a challenge he couldn't resist.

HELLO
MY NAME IS

russell sprout

Life as Mr Sprout

Russell Sprout is very happy with the change, as now everyone just calls him by the name he wants to be called, which is Sprout.

He has lost out on job opportunities because of the name change, but the council isn't bothered by it, which goes to show that public service does increase public choice and that Keynes was right. (I'm not certain that entirely encapsulates the writings of one of the twentieth century's best thinkers, but I think it does.)

Sprout Takes A Stand

Controversially, Russell Sprout does not like sprouts!

'I can't stand the things. They are the most horrible vegetable there is, apart from parsnips,' he said.

Russell, or Sprout, who is a genuinely funny man, then added, 'Anyway, it would be like eating one of your own kind.'

The Great Escape

Sprout in fact has a long history of name changes. Bridges wasn't his original surname – that was chosen at random from the phone book, in true Reggie Perrin style.

His original surname, believe it or not, was De'Ath, which he changed as soon as he was legally able: an understandable change for a fun-loving guy who'd always been nicknamed Sprout. Better than being nicknamed the Grim Reaper, I suppose, which was probably the other option.

Amazingly, De'Ath is the surname of nearly 10,000 people in Britain, and it is the country's 1,042nd most common name.

How many of these people have resorted to two surname changes, and have any others turned to sprouts to try to escape death?

savouring the sprout

So, you've heard that sprouts are good for you. You have various friends who wax lyrical about them, and you've even seen them on the menu in fancy restaurants.

You want to jump on board this brassica bus – but what if you really can't stomach sprouts? What is to be done?

Here are five top tips for retraining your palate to savour all that sprouty goodness.

The Marmite Shock Technique

For your evening meal, simply replace one of your two veg – the one that should usually be sprouts – with Marmite. Just a lake of Marmite on your plate. It's so unpleasant that soon you'll beg for Brussels.

Doublethink

You want to live healthier and actually crave the taste of good-for-you veggies like sprouts, but you can't crack the burger habit.

So, starve yourself of green vegetables in particular, and food that is good for you in general. Force your poor long-suffering body to an even more high-fat, low-nutrients diet than usual. Only white bread, no fruit, minimal beer (surprisingly nutritious stuff, beer).

If you major on bubblegum and cake for long enough, then it's quite likely that even sprouts will taste nice to you eventually.

Of course, this plan does have the downside that you may have grown to the size of a Renault Espace while waiting.

The Total Immersion Technique

Similar to the once much-vaunted – but now denounced as utter pseudo-science – method for getting people over arachnophobia, total immersion has you surviving solely on sprouts.

The claim of this theory is that it gives your body no alternative but to love sprouts.

The technique involves eating nothing except Brussels sprouts until you proclaim, 'I love sprouts!' or 'Please kill me.' Obviously, if it's the latter, you need to eat more sprouts.

The Endurance Method

You may gradually learn to like the bitter taste in some sort of culinary equivalent of a heptathlon: the seven stages of sprouts.

After all, who does not remember a baptism of fire over their first beer or coffee? 'People drink this for pleasure?'

It's the same with sprouts – it's really just a matter of willpower. The first hundred million sprouts will be the worst …

The Blindfolded Taste Test

Ask a good friend to cook up some of the tasty sprout recipes in this book, particularly Felice's children-fooling dishes, along with a few non-sprout dishes. Blindfold yourself, and then sample the fare the good friend has provided, rating the dishes as you go.

Undoubtedly, among the dishes sampled and rated highly, one or two will contain sprouts – much to your amazement. Welcome to the sprout side.

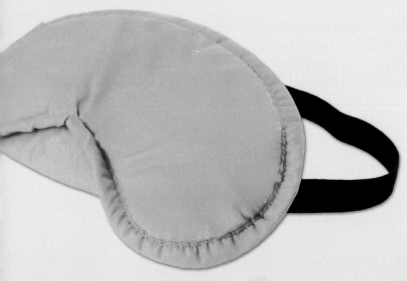

BRUSSELS SPROUTS IN BEER • *Serves 4*

You will need:
4 rashers of streaky bacon • 500 g sprouts
150 ml light beer • 150 ml apple juice

1. Cut the bacon into matchstick-sized strips.
2. Put the strips into a heavy-bottomed frying pan and cook gently until the bacon fat starts to flow (about 5 minutes).
3. Chop the sprouts in half. Once the bacon fat is flowing, put the sprouts into the pan. Cook them in the fat for 5–10 minutes until they are beginning to soften, stirring regularly.
4. Pour in the beer, turn up the heat to bubble off the alcohol, and then add the apple juice, making sure there is not so much liquid that it covers the sprouts.
5. Turn the heat back down and allow the sprouts to braise for 20 minutes; after which time, half the liquid will have evaporated down to a yummy sticky sauce coating the sprouts and the bacon, and the dish is ready to go.
6. Serve with pork or other hearty roast meat.

more imaginative things to do with sprouts

• •

Just when you thought inspiration had run dry, a whole new world of sprout-related pleasure opens up …

A Wedding Hair Piece
Good for one day only. If that.

1. Remove the outer leaves from a Brussels sprout, then take off about 6 or 7 inner tender leaves.
2. Bake these in the oven for around 10 minutes at 150°C, until they are crisp.
3. Allow the leaves to cool, then sew or glue them on to a hair comb in an attractive fashion, if such a result is possible.

Make Your Own Brussels Sprouts Jewellery

You can use the baked leaves to make a necklace, too, but beware that the feeling of browned Brussels sprouts on your skin is not usually considered a pleasant one, whereas it's just about bearable in your hair.

Brussels Sprouts Daisy Chains

Not so much something for a perfect summer's afternoon in the park, as something for an overly long day at the allotment. The result is a piece of jewellery that is absolutely conversation stopping. And not in a good way.

This activity has two disadvantages to traditional daisy chain making:

- Rather than working with pretty little daisy flowers, you are working with Brussels sprouts.
- Whereas with daisy chains all you need are the daisies, with Brussels Sprouts Daisy Chains you need to bring some kit with you.

You will need:

1 strong long needle

1 reel of strong thread, preferably plastic Silko thread (which you can usually only find in specialist haberdashers)

1 thimble, to protect your fingers from the strong needle

1. Remove the outer leaves from the sprouts.
2. Thread several sprouts together, piercing through the bottom. It requires considerable strength to pull the needle through each sprout, but to quote someone who is mad enough to have tried this activity, 'That's all part of the fun!'

Create Christmas Presents for People You Don't Like

Any of the above would be good for this really, but books describing how to make presents such as these are even better.

103

FELICE TOCCHINI'S 'SPROUTSLAW'
Makes 4 side portions

This salad will take a little longer to prepare than normal coleslaw, but the result is certainly worth the extra time. It is at its best if prepared a couple of hours before serving. It goes extremely well with cold meats and will complement a roast-beef sandwich to perfection.

You will need:
250 g sprouts • 80 g carrots, grated
1/2 onion, thinly sliced • 3 tbsp mayonnaise
1 tbsp horseradish sauce • 1 tbsp vinegar
Salt and pepper to taste

1. Wash and thoroughly clean the sprouts. Cut them into thin shreds and add to the rest of the vegetables.
2. Add the mayonnaise, horseradish sauce, and vinegar. Mix together well and season to taste.

grow, grow, grow your sprouts
• • • • • • • • • • • • • • • •

If you're considering growing
sprouts, here are some top tips.

Think Big

Plant your seeds in as large an area
as you can. Brassicas like lots of air
circulating around their leaves (and
don't we all …?) and really prefer a
big wild open space to a garden.

Whatever an overly ambitious
Sunday supplement may tell you –
you *cannot* grow sprouts from a
window box.

Know The Enemy

There are a-thousand-and-one
dangers for the would-be sprout-
grower, although as yet there has
been no *March of the Penguins*-

style documentary showing the dangerous journey of sprouts toward adulthood.

The most important piece of advice for a potential sprout-grower is to make sure your initial sprout seedlings don't have clubroot. This is the deadly enemy of sprouts (hence the excitement over the potential first sighting of clubroot in art, page 82).

did you know?

The processes from seeding to harvesting Brussels sprouts take up to 100 days, so to get your sprouts on Christmas Day, you should be sowing seeds in early to mid September.

Lavender Green

Brassicas grow quite like lavender does – which is to say, treat them mean and they will thrive.

This is so true for brassicas that botanists, who had noticed that wild cabbages by the sea grew particularly strong and healthy, decided to treat their land-lubbing brassica cousins to a salty snack each winter – a course of action still believed by many to be beneficial.

The Exception to the Rule

However, Bob Herbert of the National Vegetable Society observes, 'The only exception to this is the cauliflower, which can be regarded as the queen of brassicas and, as befits a lady, should be treated more delicately.'

The sprout, on the other hand, is no lady. Another reason, if any was needed, to grow sprouts instead of cauliflower.

did you know?

The supermarkets aim to get sprouts from the fields to the shops in 18–24 hours.

VARIETIES OF SPROUT

Widgeon

Sheriff

Nelson

Falstaff

Cambridge No. 5
(not to be confused with
Chanel No. 5 …)

sprouts in the record books

● ●

> Sprouts-eating record:
> Forty-three in one minute
> How did he do it?

Dave Mynard set this verified *Guinness World Records* record for Brussels sprouts eating at the Cactus Television Studios in London on 10 December 2003, and it still stands today, despite others' attempts to better it.

Attempts at Glory

Richard Townsend from Exeter, for example, tried to be a record-breaker in December 2006, but failed, managing to chomp only thirty-seven sprouts in the same time. He explained his defeat afterwards in this way: 'I just lost it.'

He went on to say, 'I don't think I could face another sprout for a few days,' but then, when the excitement had died down, he ate a few more, saying it seemed a shame to waste them. The man likes his sprouts.

The Biggest Sprout in the World?

In December 2006, market gardener Carol Farley, of Culm Valley Organics, Devon, discovered in her family's acre of growing sprouts one massive sprout, nestling next to its normal-sized siblings.

The sprout was genuinely huge – weighing nearly one-and-a-half pounds, which is to say, fifty times heavier than the average sprout.

It was also considerably bigger than the head of Carol's four-year-old nephew, Joshua (pictured).

The Farley family, probably very wisely, decided not to eat it for Christmas dinner. Instead, they turned it into the table's centerpiece. Inspired.

Mr Big

Yet the Farleys' monster sprout was nowhere near the size of the *Guinness World Records*' winning sprout.

That dubious honour goes to a sprout grown in 1992, which weighed an extraordinary 18 lb 3 oz and was produced by Bernard Lavery of Llanharry, near Bridgend.

FELICE TOCCHINI'S FARFALLE AI CAVOLINI E OLIO
Serves 6

The success of this dish depends entirely on using extremely good extra virgin olive oil, as well as some basic cooking competence.

You will need:
500 g farfalle pasta • 75 ml extra virgin olive oil
2 cloves of garlic, crushed • 1 chilli, crushed
250 g sprouts, finely sliced • Salt and pepper, pinch of each
50 g Parmesan shavings

1. Bring a pot of salted water to the boil. Drop in the pasta, stirring occasionally, and cook for the time directed on the packet for an al dente finish.
2. In a large sauté pan, pour in half of the oil, add the garlic and chilli and cook until golden.
3. Add the sprouts and cook for a further 3 minutes, stirring constantly.
4. Drain the pasta and toss with the sauce.
5. Add the rest of the oil, season and then serve immediately, topped with the shavings of Parmesan.

kids and sprouts

Whoever heard of a child liking Brussels sprouts? Surely it has never been known. Popular folklore has it that children are morally opposed to eating up their greens and that Brussels sprouts are substantially to blame for greens in general getting a bad press from the under-ten market segment.

So, we took the fight to the enemy (in this case, children) and went to Hawley Infants School in Camden, north London, armed with sprouts for tasting and a verbal sprout survey. How would the kids react?

Christopher Robin lookalike Joe (left) and friend Jacques with their sprout pictures.

The Survey

Four six-year-old girls put up their hands enthusiastically to the question: 'Who here has eaten sprouts?' One, a pale girl with sweet brown hair and funky clothing, even announced: 'I love sprouts, they are my favourite vegetable. Sprouts and cauliflower.' Well, it takes all sorts.

So to the second question: 'And who here doesn't like sprouts?'

Numerous hands shot up and many anxious eyes turned to the tasting bowls.

And then I asked a rather more basic question, which presumably should have come first: 'And who has never heard of sprouts or doesn't know what they are?'

A clear majority of the class raised their hands in answer to this question – including, of course, several of the children who had earlier agreed that they certainly didn't like them.

I then asked jokily, 'And how many of you are scared of sprouts?'

Many hands went skywards.

> **'I ate all my sprouts and asked for seconds.'**
>
> Perfect Peter, brother to Horrid Henry, both creations of Francesca Simon

The Sprouts

The teachers loved the sprouts. Genuinely could not get enough of them, and literally asked for the recipes, which happily are to be found in this very book.

The extraordinary thing was, the dishes were also a hit with many of the children. Not only the ones who didn't like sprouts *before* the tastings, but also those who said they didn't *afterwards*. Their words, and this was many more than just one child, were: 'I didn't like the sprouts, I only liked the pasta.'

But, of course – and this was the truly shocking part to all concerned – there was no pasta, only shredded sprouts cooked in orange juice (see page 122 for the recipe).

Sprout Gallery

Following the survey and the sprout-eating session, the children let loose their creative talents. The results are reproduced on the following pages.

Child Geniuses

Admire Jacques's complicated picture, in which the sun is happy because the rain on the Brussels sprouts will (somewhat contrary to the laws of nature) stop them growing.

How reminiscent of Ford Maddox Ford, author and friend of Ezra Pound, on the climate of Provence: 'Oh blessed land, where the apple is seldom seen and the Brussels sprout will not grow at all.'

Then there's Fred's extraordinary picture, which would certainly have got on to Tony Hart's gallery, unless he was excluded on the assumption that the picture must clearly have been drawn by his parents/overly ambitious art teacher, which I can testify that it wasn't.

'Disgusting,' said the sun. The sun doesn't want the Brussels sprouts to grow because I don't like them. That's why it's raining in my picture. And I am the sun, my friend Joe is the sun too.

Jacques, aged 6

Happy smiling sprouts keeping fit.

Matthew, aged 7

A Brussels sprout man, eating sprouts from a sprouty mountain.

Bluebelle, aged 6

A bird, a man with a dog on a lead and a creature fight over a Brussels sprout. The eternal battle. Who will win?

Fred, aged 7

A Christmas tree decorated with Brussels sprouts.

Makaeda, aged 7

Char lar lar / Boom-dee-ay / My Brussels sprout flew away. / It came back yesterday. / It was on holiday. (They went to Australia as we can see from the hats.)

Archie, aged 7

Brussels sprouts begging for mercy, but getting none.

Vincent, aged 7

Children Also Write Damn Fine Poems

They really do. Or is it just that the painstaking researchers of this book have tracked down two of the country's most talented young poetic writers? And they are both sisters. Of each other. And to make it even better, one hates sprouts and one loves them. So without further ado, here is their work.

Rachel kicks off the argument.

B is for Brussel sprouts!
R is for revolting!
U is for ugly veg!
S is for slimy!
S is for slippery greens!
E is for Eurgh!
L is for loads of leaves!

S is for soggy!
P is for painful taste!
R is for rubbish!
O is for 'orrible stuff!
U is for unmistakable!
T is for terrible torture!
You know what ... Brussel sprouts!

120

But Emma fights back:

Brussels sprouts taste so yummy,
Brussels sprouts are so scrummy,
Brussels sprouts are so delicious,
Brussels sprouts are also nutritious.
Mmm … I love Brussels sprouts!

Rachel delivers the killer blow:

Green and slimy
Wet and slippery
Children whiny
Parents grumbling
Chop, sizzle, chop, chop …
I hate Brussels sprouts!

i think it's safe to say
she's not a fan of sprouts.

STIR-FRIED SPROUTS WITH ORANGE JUICE • *Serves 4*

You will need:

500 g sprouts
1 tsp oil
150 ml orange juice
Salt and pepper to taste

1. Prepare the sprouts by washing them and removing the outer leaves.
2. Shred the sprouts by cutting the 'stalk' off each one, and then slicing them into vertical strips, leaving you with about 450 grams of loose shreds of sprout foliage.
3. Heat the oil in a wok or frying pan until it is just below smoking point, then throw in the sprouts. Stir them rapidly (otherwise the ones at the bottom will burn) and allow them to cook through for 5 minutes.
4. Add the orange juice, which will boil and splutter, and remove immediately from the heat. Keep stirring for about 30 seconds to distribute the half-evaporated orange juice through the sprouts, then season and serve.

inspirational sprouts

There are many wonderful examples of sprouts in all aspects of culture – well, examples anyway.

Sprouts have inspired the following artists to new creative heights.

Magda Clark, a living artist based in England, specializes in portraits of vegetables, including aubergines, mushrooms, peppers, garlic, shallots and, of course, sprouts.

Prefab Sprout, the rock band of the 1980s, who conjured up images of prefabricated Brussels sprouts and produced such songs as 'Lions in My Own Garden' and 'Green Isaac' (could this be another sprout reference?), were frequently asked why they chose that name for their group.

The answer was always rather unsatisfactory – it was a bit like the names of other successful bands of the time, such as the Rolling Stones. But more sprouty, presumably.

Author **Robert Rankin** took inspiration from the world of brassicas when he decided that the 'fourth part' of his 'Brentford Trilogy' should be called *The Sprouts of Wrath*.

This book followed other notable successes for Rankin such as *The Witches of Chiswick*, *East of Ealing*, *Sex and Drugs and Sausage Rolls*. No, I'm not making this stuff up, Rankin is.

A one-act comedy entitled *A Need for Brussels Sprouts* emerged in the 1980s, written by **Murray Schisgal**. The show portrayed a domestic set-to between a noisy neighbour and the policewoman who books him for it, whom he then tries to seduce.

Brussels sprouts played a surprisingly small role in the play, and took only a brief curtain call at the end.

American harpist **Joanna Newsom** wrote a song called 'Sprout and the Bean', which explores the nature of the difference between the two. Apparently, the difference is a 'golden ring', and a 'twisted string'.

Sprout Limericks

Sprouts really are inspirational. People say there's a limerick for every occasion, but here are three on the subject of sprouts.

There once was a nun from Siberia,
Who juggled sprouts on her posterior.
The convent was rapt,
They all cheered and clapped,
And now she's the Mother Superior.

There once was a woman from Fleet,
Who ate Brussels sprouts with her feet.
A man from *The Sun*,
Came round at the run,
And now she's the talk of Fleet Street.

A Brussels sprouts fan from Darjeeling,
Gobbled sprouts with incredible feeling.
They all said, 'We implore
You to eat off the floor,'
But he stubbornly ate off the ceiling.

sprouts' revenge
●●

And so, with a heavy heart and a baleful eye on the sniggerers at the back of the class, we finally depart from our serious culinary exposition and venture on to the subject which no doubt nine out of ten readers have bought the book for ... Go on, better out than in, admit you want to ask it ...

Do Sprouts Make You Fart?
Yes, they do. Are you happy now? Sprouts make you fart. It's a medical fact. Want to know more? Of course you do.

did you know?
There is a variety of sprouts, and it's a popular variety too, called Revenge.

The Make-Up of a Fart
Flatulence in humans (and other animals, but most other animals don't eat sprouts) has two elements:

1. The gas. This is generally hydrogen, carbon dioxide or methane, produced by various kinds of bacteria that live in the digestive system (the 'intestinal flora').

2. The smell. Hydrogen and methane are both odourless gases so, rather like a fine red wine, the 'bouquet' of a fart is produced by small traces of volatile compounds, which are carried to the nose in the gaseous cloud.

Sprouts are something of a 'perfect storm' of flatulence-inducing food, having chemical properties that make them well placed to supply both the 'missile' and the 'warhead'.

For a majestic quote on wind, this superlative exchange between Winston Churchill and F. E. Smith (obscure politician of the day) trumps the lot:

F. E. Smith, satirically suggesting that Winston was so fat that he looked pregnant: Congratulations, Winston, what are you going to call it?'

Churchill: If it's a boy, I shall call it John. If it's a girl, I shall call it Mary. But if, as I suspect, it's trapped wind, I shall call it F. E. Smith.

The Missile

Sprouts contain raffinose, a complex carbohydrate that is also found in beans, cabbage, asparagus, Jerusalem artichokes, and other foodstuffs that also ought to have a 'Flatulence' section in any books written about them.

The Fuse

Lots of people, apparently, lack the enzymes necessary to digest raffinose in the small intestine; among these people, a significant proportion also lack the intestinal bacteria which might resolve the problem in the large intestine. The two deficits combined lead directly to excess gas.

did you know?

Doctors attempting to treat excessive gas (and by the way, it has to be really excessive before most doctors will treat your flatulence as their business) will advise cutting sprouts and other brassicas out of your diet as a first step.

The Warhead

Of course, sprouts could cause you to produce enough hydrogen to reflate the R101 and nobody would care if it didn't smell (apart from a few unfortunate victims of bloating and/or spontaneous combustion).

Now, the one thing that smells worse than nearly anything in the world is hydrogen sulphide (a compound contained in rotten eggs and stink bombs).

As it happens, the sulphur compounds that give sprouts their characteristic flavour often react with hydrogen in the intestine to form hydrogen sulphide – as well as all sorts of other evil-smelling compounds … thus ensuring that not only are sprout-induced farts copious, but that they smell, too.

The Target

So in summary, they're a really good food to leave out for the dog of the neighbour that you don't like.

The Kraken Wakes

In 2006, a sea turtle in a sea life centre in Dorset was given a Christmas treat of Brussels sprouts – with predictable, but apparently unforeseen, consequences.

Shortly after the turtle ate the sprouts, the alarm on the turtle's tank went off. A nearby marine biologist rushed to the centre, assuming the tank was overflowing and the creatures were in peril.

All seemed well, but there were bubbles on the water's surface. Why? And why had the alarm gone off?

As more bubbles appeared, the highly trained crew realized that the bubbles had popped on the water's surface and splashed water on to a sensor, and that the bubbles were there because, er, the turtle had farted.

Q: Why don't cannibals eat weathermen?

A: Because it gives them wind. So do sprouts.

FERMENTED PICKLED SPROUTS ('SAUERSPRAUT')
Makes 1.5 kg of Sauerspraut (roughly 12 servings)

WARNING:
THIS IS 'EXTREME' SPROUT COOKERY

Homemade pickles of this sort always run a (small) risk that if the jar and equipment aren't sterilized properly, the anaerobic conditions under which the fermentation takes place are also perfect for the bacteria which cause botulism to grow. Botulism from home pickling and canning kills about three or four people a year in the developed world.

So, sterilize everything properly, throw away any pickles that appear to have grown mouldy or slimy, and indeed ask yourself the question: 'Am I really prepared to risk actual death in order to eat pickled sprouts?'

Another important note is that you need to use equal proportions of normal cabbage with sprouts. White cabbage has more sugar and liquid in it and as a result will ferment properly; a sauerspraut made purely with sprouts will just rot down to a slimy mess.

You will need:

1 kg white cabbage
1 kg sprouts
4 tbsp sea salt
Water and salt for extra brine
A large (2.5 litre) earthenware pot
A large weight - a big plate with a
rock on top, a freezer bag full of water,
or something else: the best choice will
depend on the shape of your pot.

**SPROUTINESS
RATING: 1.5/5**

It has a pleasant sharpness
to it – the taste of the sprouts
is there, but not particularly
intensely.

**KRAUTINESS
RATING: 5/5**

Not everyone likes sauerkraut
and that's what this is.

1. Wash and shred the cabbage and the sprouts. (It's best to do this in batches in a food processor because it's important to get them chopped very thin.)
2. Put the shredded vegetables in your earthenware pot and mix in the salt with a wooden spoon. Keep mixing until a salty 'juice' starts to flow out of the cabbage.
3. Press the cabbage and sprouts down in the pot and see if there is enough juice to cover the vegetables. Because you're using equal proportions of sprouts, which have less water in them, there probably won't be, so top up the jar with some more brine (you can make brine of the right strength by dissolving 1 tablespoon of sea salt in 1 litre of water). Add brine until it just covers the cabbage/sprout mixture.

4. Now use your large weight to press down the sauerspraut as it ferments. Place the weight directly on top of your sauerspraut, then cover the top of the pot with cling film. You want to get an airtight seal so that it will ferment, rather than growing mould from airborne spores.
5. Put the pot in a cool, dark place and leave it there for three weeks, then unwrap and remove the weight.

IMPORTANT NOTE:

If it looks like it might have grown a botulism culture, throw it away.

While there are some books on pickling that suggest that a thin layer of pale mould on top is all right and just needs to be scraped off, this book is not one of them. After all, who wants to eat mouldy pickled sprouts?

tip

If you put some Korean spices and chillis in during the pickling stage, you could probably make sprout kimchi, but now you really are on your own.

6. Pour off the brine and enjoy.

love: sprout style

• • • • • • • • • • • • • • • • • • • •

Ooh. At last we address the long history of sprouts as aphrodisiacs. Yes, it started with the *Sexing Up the Sprout* programme in 2004 and it may not have finished yet.

If you're tempted to cover your lover in sprouts instead of rose petals à la *American Beauty*, you're not the first. Advertising agency Taylor Herring used just such a shot to promote the aforementioned sexy sprout TV series (see overleaf).

Let's Get It On

For the sprout aficionado in your life, here's how to blow their socks/rocks off.

Kick off the evening with sproutinis to make sure they're good and drunk – they'll need to be to face the evening ahead.

Then serve a good sprout-based menu like a roast served with bacon and sprouts, followed by Sprouty

Cake, with Felice Tocchini's 'British Sprouts' and Chestnut Soup (see overleaf) to start.

Line the path to the bedroom with sprouts.

Why Stop There?
Let your imagination run wild – sprouts passed from mouth to mouth, sprouts to create artificially (or naturally, depending on how you think about it) large nipples that can be lovingly nibbled upon, sprout leaves spilled across the skin in a sensual sprouty trail …

The Finishing Touch
Arranging scented sprouts on your lover's pillows at night would send tremors through any bosom. Possibly even in a good way.

FELICE TOCCHINI'S 'BRITISH SPROUTS' AND CHESTNUT SOUP • *Serves 6*

You will need:

1 medium onion, chopped

2 white leeks, rinsed and chopped

40 g butter • 300 g sprouts, trimmed

2 small potatoes, peeled and diced

1 litre vegetable stock • Salt and pepper • 4 rashers of smoked bacon

100 g chestnuts, blanched, peeled and crumbled

Whipping cream, for garnish

1. Sweat the onion and leeks in the butter, then add the sprouts and potatoes and cook for a further 10 minutes.
2. Add the vegetable stock and cook on a low heat for 40 minutes.
3. Pour the soup into a food processor or liquidizer. Blend until smooth. Then return the soup to the rinsed-out pan, reheat gently and adjust for seasoning.
4. In the meantime, dice the bacon and cook with a little oil until very crispy. Drain the pieces and place on to paper towels to remove all the grease.
5. Pour the soup into bowls, garnish with some of the bacon and chestnuts, and finish with a swirl of cream.

epilogue: the author's tale

Of course, I hated sprouts as a child. They were the freshest, greenest, brightest things from my wonderful grandfather's allotment. They were horrible. Truly horrible. But so were all vegetables, except marrowfat peas.

But then I grew, and as sherbet lost its allure, so tomatoes became interesting, then leeks, then mushrooms, finally broccoli. But there was still a sticking point over sprouts.

Why? Was it because the memory of the smell was still too much, or simply because on the no-smoke-without-fire principle, there had to be something wrong with them as they get such bad press?

Well, friends – brothers, even – become vegetarian and at some point in life you just can't go on avoiding vegetables on the grounds of squeamishness. So they had to be tried.

Actually, they weren't that bad. Yes, still sprouty of old, but nutty too, and good and crunchy, and green like broccoli, and, well, delicious. And before I knew what had happened, I was writing a book about the things and tramping the streets of London late on Sunday nights, desperately trying to find sprouts to cook to cure a sudden craving.

Unsuccessfully, I should add. Damn those Sunday trading laws.

Now I find that sprouts have given me so much: hours of pleasure from eating, cooking, writing. And not only that. While researching the Brussels connection for Brussels sprouts, I suddenly find on an obscure French website the telephone number for a long-lost native Brussels friend, whom I had tried to track down so many times. She looks just the same and has also developed a love of sprouts – we shall meet in Paris and celebrate the old times and the new.

As if that weren't enough, I'm now known to all my son's friends as 'the Brussels sprouts lady'.

author's acknowledgements

Thanks are very much due to:

Danny, Joe, Poppy, Glendra, the Brussels Sprouts Growers' Association, Felice Tocchini and everyone at Fusion Brasserie, Kate Gribble, Lindsay Davies, Shane Osborn, the National Gallery of Scotland, Howard Drury, Robin Illingworth, Tom Raymond, Rachel, Emma, and not forgetting Michelle and Ben for their favourite super sprout recipes (the Sprout and Potato Cakes recipe and the Stir-Fried Christmas Dinner Sprouts with Soy Sauce recipe respectively).

Also to everyone at Hawley Infants School in Camden: Anne Fontaine, Jasbir, Raz, Godfrey, and all the kids in Year One: Joe, Jacques, Bluebelle, Aison, Max, Nina, Alexandra, Alex, Lottie, Betty, Ayesha, Joel, Jezz, Edie, Biba, Shayama, Dujana, Sarah, Savina, Maya, Mela, Vesa and Layana; and Year Two: Minnie, Lily, Fred, Vincent, Shannon, Lucy, Archie, Matthew, Gabriel, Bessie, Ellie, Makaeda, Emily, Adrian, Luca, Ellen, Sima and Kayleigh.

Finally, thanks to Mel Harris, whose passion for sprouts made this book happen.

picture acknowledgements

● ●

A J Sokainer/Rex Features p. 50

Andrew Twort/Red Cover/Getty Images p. 19

© Digital Vision Ltd/Superstock pp. 32-33, 34, 42

© Simon Colner and Abby Rex/Alamy pp. 20-21, 100-101 (sprouts)

David Fisher/Rex Features p. 51 (above)

Jonathan Player/Rex Features p. 63

Richard Saker/Rex Features p. 53 (right)

Richard Waitt, *The Cromartie Fool*, Scottish National Portrait Gallery p. 81

Stills Press Agency/Rex Features p. 124

Stuart Clarke/Rex Features p. 62

Theo Moye/apexnewspix.com, with kind permission of Culm Valley Organic Vegetables, Uffculme, Devon p. 110

Tom Grill/Iconica/Getty Images p. 12

www.alexisdubus.co.uk pp. 30-31 (background), 42 (bars), 46 (below), 53 (right), 59, 61, 64, 67, 71, 73, 84, 104, 112, 139

www.iStockphoto.com pp. 16, 26, 29, 43, 46 (above), 76, 96-97, 100-101, 108, 120-121, 135

www.shutterstock.com pp. 11, 14-15, 16, 22, 23, 25, 32-33 (centre), 34 (above left), 37, 38, 40-41, 47, 50 (above) 51 (below both), 52 (left), 53 (left), 54, 57, 68-69, 75, 77, 78, 80, 83, 87, 88-89, 93, 94, 98, 99, 100-101 (daisies), 102, 106, 111, 123, 131

Cartoon on p. 49 by kind courtesy of Nick D Kim/nearingzero.net

Image on p. 136-137 reproduced by kind courtesy of UKTV Food/Taylor Herring Public Relations Ltd. Image supplied by Mirrorpix.